Black Sketchbooks

London Adam & Charles Black

PUBLISHED BY
A. & C. BLACK · SOHO SQUARE · LONDON W.

BRIGHTON
& ENVIRONS

A SKETCH~BOOK
by H·G·Hampton &
Dorothy E·G·Woollard

A·&·C·BLACK·LTD·LONDON·W·1919

WEST STREET

KING'S ROAD

WEST PIER.

PALACE PIER

KING'S CLIFF

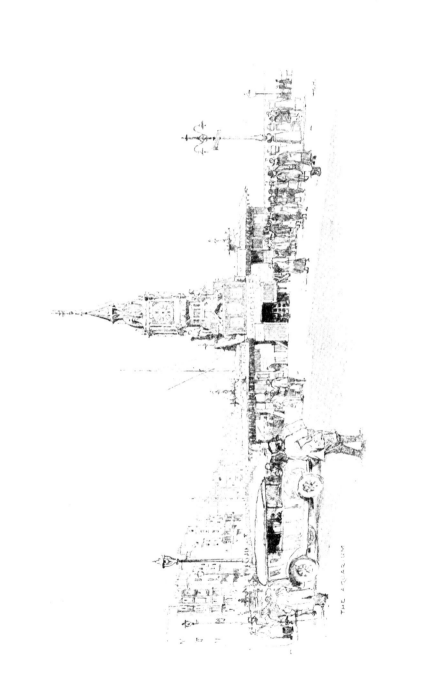

THE AQUARIUM

THE OLD STEINE FROM PALACE PIER

THE OLD STEINE GARDENS

THE ROYAL PAVILION

MARKET STREET

THE OLD BUN SHOP·POOL VALLEY

MEETING HOUSE LANE

ST. PETER'S CHURCH

BRIGHTON COLLEGE

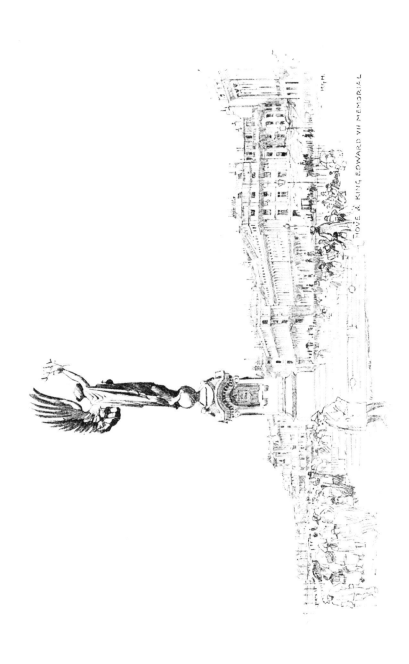

HOVE & KING EDWARD VII MEMORIAL

BLACK ROCK

ROTTINGDEAN

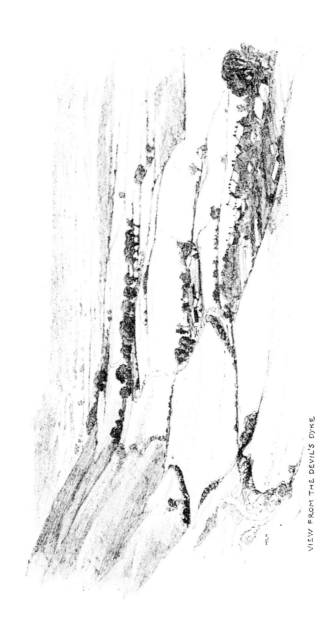

VIEW FROM THE DEVIL'S DYKE

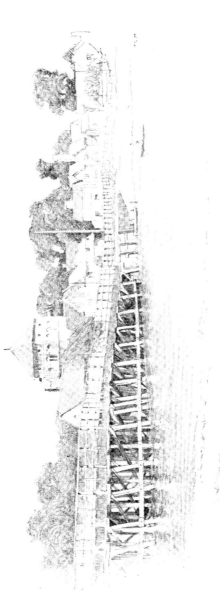

OLD SHOREHAM

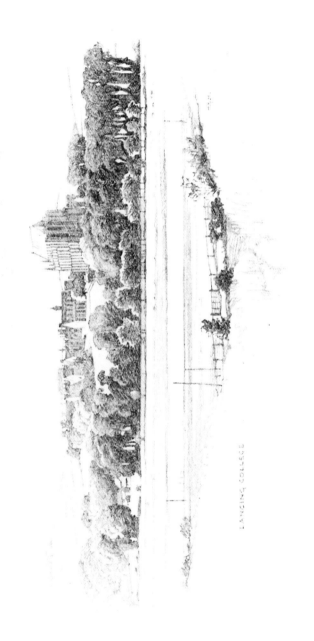

LANSING COLLEGE.

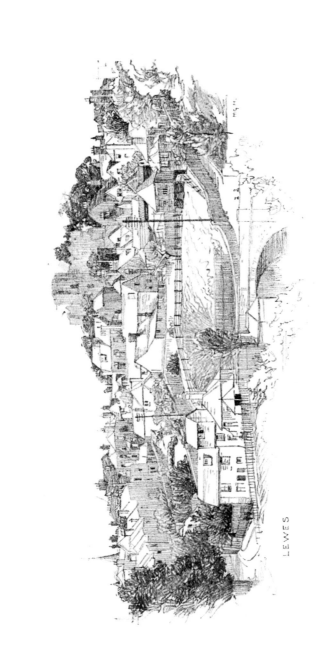

LEWES

THE BARBICAN
LEWES CASTLE

BRAMBER

First published in Great Britain in 1919
by A&C Black Publishers
36 Soho Square
London W1D 3QY
www.acblack.com

This edition published 2009

© 1919, 2009 A&C Black

ISBN 978-1-408-11557-2

A CIP record of this book is available from the British Library

Printed and bound in China